Sun of the Souls

Payel Sanyal

Published by "The Great Indian Book Tour"
Imprint : Holistic Publishing
www.tgibt.com

Title : **Sun of the Souls**
Author : **Payel Sanyal**
Copyright © Payel Sanyal 2022
All rights reserved

First published in 2022
First Edition 2022

ISBN : 978-93-93262-11-0

Thank You

I would like to express my gratitude towards people, without whom I would not be the person I am today.

I would like to say "THANK YOU" to all of my readers, who keep me inspired to write.

I would like to say "THANK YOU" to all the creative personalities of the world who keep us alive so that we can lead our lives in a better way.

"THANK YOU" to all the collaborative authors in my life –

My parents

My teachers

My friends

I would like to say "THANK YOU" to the team of The Great Indian Book Tour Publishing, who brought my story to the world.

I would like to say "THANK YOU" to all the people whom I met through the journey of my life till now.

Dedicated to

Singer Somlata Acharyya Chowdhury

Contents

2022

X = Y

"Good morning, my star."

"Um… Let me sleep for fifteen minutes, Mani."

"You need to wake up within five minutes."

"Let me sleep for another five minutes, naa. Please don't disturb, else even those precious five minutes will be gone."

Tiyasha laughs at the words of this girl. She checked the time. It was 5:05 am.

"Wake up, Ananya."

"Tiash… come and have your tea."

"Coming.", she replies loudly to mom.

"You go. I will wake up. Don't make elders wait for you." Ananya says, turning to another side of the bed for another five minute nap.

"Junior, wake up fast…." she just pulls her blanket up and goes to have tea.

"Mani…." she feels irritated and finally wakes up.

She is getting freshened up and ready to go out with Tiyasha.

"Didun, give me breakfast."

Mom finished her tea and went to the kitchen to get her breakfast.

"Mani, where is Nish?" Tiyasha asked.

"Have it" said mom giving her breakfast, "Babu is sleeping."

"Why did he come sooooo early from his office, Didun?"

"He had headache." she feels worried for her son.

Ananya finishes her breakfast and comes to my room.

"Nish…."

"Junior, don't wake him up naa.

Tiyasha appears behind her and says, "Let him rest."

"Tiash, I am awake. Trying to sleep. Star, tell me, what's up?"

"Good morning, I came to check on you."

Tiyasha smiles at her junior's cuteness.

"Good morning. Now, go with Mani." I replied, with a good-morning hug to my star.

"Are you ready with your kit?"

"Yes."

"You disturbed my sleep by yanking my blanket. When you call me, I wake up naa. Why did you pull my blanket? I don't like it."

"Oh really? Do you wake up immediately after I call you?"

"Yes."

"Achha bachhu. I will check it from next day. Now, let's go."

They reached the cricket ground at 5:45 am. Every day, coaching starts at 6:00 am. Ananya loves to play cricket. Every morning, either me or Tiyasha take her to the Cricket Coaching Academy.

Tiyasha -Ananya -Me: Our equations are out of the scope of any biological relationship but within the syllabus of blood relations, as we all have the same color of blood.

Each equation with each of the three is

$$X=Y$$

Where, X represents humanity and Y represents an unconditional relationship.

RAINBOW OF SUCCESS

"Good morning everyone. I am Tiyasha Roy. I am a team member of our Quality Assurance Team. Today I am here for my team to appreciate their hard work. We are part of our organization, and our organization has achieved its highest turn-over. Members of all other teams, along with our team, are the equal contributors to the success of our company."

Tiyasha Roy works as a quality assurance professional for a pharmaceutical manufacturing organization in Visakhapatnam.

"Manufacturing units of medicine are in operating conditions for 24*7 hours to be of service to our customers. Our customers are our patients. Our sole goal is to produce medicine by keeping the betterment of our patient's life in our mind..

I am going to present our team's struggles and successes by a PowerPoint presentation with the support of our IT team."

I see her as a team leader with high energy and emotions towards her team members, holding a microphone on the stage, presenting the diligent story of the contributors to this success.

"This presentation will show how we overcame those struggles and achieved the desired target. Still, I know that this presentation is not sufficient to value their hard work, as it will only give some digits of the achieved target. I am not able to quantify their diligence.

I want to unfold the story of my team's hard work and their dedication, which made some impossible milestones possible and helped our organization achieve success."

Today is a vital day for her career as she is representing her team as well as our whole production unit in front of the top officials, who came from Mumbai. They congratulated all the employees of our units in Visakhapatnam for their huge business turnover.

Yesterday, I asked Tiyasha, "What does success mean to you?"

"I move one step forward from my existing position, and my move makes at least one person move forward from their current position. This is my success."

Tiyasha replied in between her work, "See, Anish, success is a very relative term for me. Today I am successful. After some years, someone will take my place. Better to focus on doing my work diligently and dedicatedly; the rest of all things will fall into their own place."

"Let's go for some coffee." Rakesh called me. He is my team member. I checked the time and it was 4:47 pm.

Everyone is celebrating their success at the company premises. The presentation session is over.

When our diligence shows the rainbow of success, we feel content inside us. I know what I feel is felt by others too.

CHAPTERS OF INSPIRATION

My phone rings, and it is Ananya.

"Nish, how is Mani's presentation?"

"It is going on."

"Had your food?"

"It's done."

"Okay. Take rest."

With her naughty tone, she disconnects the call "Ooookkkay".

She is twelve years old. She came from her school and checked on Tiyasha. She tries to take care of us at this young age. It makes me very happy for my star.

Let me introduce myself quickly. I am Anish Mukherjee. I hail from Vizag and work as a Pharmaceutical Manufacturing Specialist.

"Tiash, how was the presentation?", she sits in the cafeteria, writing the details of today's activities and listening to the song **"Pratisruti"** from the Bengali music album, "Pratisruti", playing from her mobile.

"If we really understand each and every interpretation of this song and try to implement the same in our real life, we can find peace everywhere, and most importantly, within ourselves also." She had once shared her feelings towards this song.

"Everyone is appreciating your presentation as well as you as a leader. Are you happy?"

"Yes, obviously, I am happy. Thank you for the compliment."

I tried to achieve my objective and said the same during my presentation also. Now the audience should respond. I will be waiting for their feedback. And my team is my strength. I appreciate each one of them. Kudos to their tenacious work."

"Your work and consistency will be the voice of your success. You will celebrate your success and begin working quietly and diligently toward your next goal while keeping your feet on the ground. You connect to people through both your work and your words. You always remain true to your work – this attitude helps you to achieve success.

This learning emerges from the chapters of inspiration of my life, Anish."

She tells me and leaves the cafeteria with a smile.

Tiyasha is silent but connected to the people. You will not find her in chaos but in the quiet zone of the chaotic zone.

A BEAM OF RAYS

We work in rotational shifts. For morning shifts, I wake up around 5 am. Then I take my star to her cricket coaching academy. From there, I go to company on my bike.

Tiyasha takes Ananya to practice cricket, when I am working in the night shift or the second shift. She also works in shifts like me except night shift. We try to manage our shifts in such a way so that anyone of us can spend time with her.

"Hello, Tiash, what are you doing?"

I called her entering the house from my morning shift.

"We are having a cricket tournament in our company. Just practicing for it."

"How is your practice going? Are you batting or bowling?"

"I am doing both. I will go after the first wicket goes down."

"Okay, so, that means, our all-rounder madam will come to the ground in third position as per your team's batting order. Right?"

"Don't act like as if you don't understand anything."

I laughed. I love to irritate her sometimes.

"Tiash, who is the captain of your team?"

"Nitya Arora, your dear friend." She laughed loudly.

"Why are you laughing?"

"Nothing, I just laughed that."

"Oye, there is nothing in my mind about her. I like her work. She is my colleague. That's all."

"Is it so?" Tiyasha laughed mischievously.

"Shut up. Don't be so happy about this. Stop laughing, idiot."

"Be cool, man. Tell me, where is Ananya? What is she doing?"

"She is in another room."

"Go and see her once."

"Okay, madam. I will check your junior."

"You take rest also. I am going back to my practice. Meet you in the evening."

I went to the next room and saw Ananya making a sketch.

"Star, what are you doing?"

"Can I ask one question?" She asked me.

"Sure."

"If you can see that I am making sketch, why you do ask me what am I doing?"

I don't have any answer to her question. She is smarter than we are.

"Okay. I understand."

"Nish, tell me, how do you know Mani?"

"She is my friend. We worked together."

"Why are you asking this?"

"Actually, Didun was on call with someone, most probably with Mani's mom, that Didun."

Ananya calls my mom 'Didun' as well as Tiyasha's mom also.

"What did they say?"

"You were overprotective of me. You fought with Mani over me. They were talking like, you know, Didun's talk."

I laugh as I had never heard this word "Didun's talk." I have heard about 'girls-talk', 'boys' talk.'

"Yes, we did fight as we love you a lot."

"Yaa, I know that, but Mani is cool and you are always tensed in every situation."

She is fully supportive of her Mani.

"Okay. Mani has her cricket tournament in our office."

"Okay."

Ananya stares at the ceiling and asks, "What is the time now?"

"5:16 pm. Why?"

She does not reply and continues with her sketching.

I just remembered that Ananya has her tuition classes today from 7:30 pm. probably it must have been the reason.

"Complete your sketch. You have your tuition classes."

"I know my Nish. Please don't get stressed. You just take an hour's nap." I blew on her head.

It will take about one hour from our house to Ananya's tuition classes. Tiyasha or me – whoever comes before her tuition classes, took our little one to her classes, and she returned with her friends or sometimes either me or Tiyasha go to pick her.

I went to my room to sleep for some time. .

I am listening to the tunes of the song **"Tui Chol"** from the Bengali movie "Brahma Janen Gopon Kommoti." coming from her room.

Tiyasha says, "This song is so significant to my life that when I see darkness in the days, a beam of light falls upon me and removes the curtain of darkness in my life. The illumination of that light is so bright; it sows seeds of courage inside me to face any challenges alone without expecting support from anyone."

Music is a timeless source of strength for the listeners,

GUIDING STAR

"Oi, what's up?" I came to meet my dear friend.

"Nothing. Feeling hungry and tired too."

Tiyasha sits in a restaurant. She had returned late from the company.

"I am going to order two plates of Chicken Momos."

"Okay. Done", I agree.

She is checking the news updates of the day on her mobile.

"We never thought that we could come to the restaurant again to have food or to spend some relaxation time. Do you remember those days, Anish?"

"Those were horrible days for everyone's lives in the world. Now it is somewhat getting normal and we are trying to get back to normal."

"What else can we do even? Wearing masks and using sanitizer is a mandatory part of the daily habits of our life."

"Maintain social distance as well," she adds.

Two friends are waiting for the food and remembering and talking about many things, but we know that even after many conversations, we will still have many pending talks.

"Tiash, you love to play cricket, naa?"

"Yes…I love it very much. When I was in school, I played cricket with my friends. I always imagined that I was playing for my country."

"I used to sit on our veranda when gully-cricket started after I got home from school," she continues. I observed the boys playing cricket on the street of our lane. I practiced to catch the ball with my school friends on the wall of my house."

"And obviously, aunty used to shout at you as you played inside of your house. Right, my girl?"

"Yes.", Tiash says with a smile.

"Why did not you work upon your love? Why didn't you join a Cricket Academy for coaching?"

"Frankly speaking, my family did not have that required amount of money to pay for my cricket coaching classes. They were bearing all expenses regarding my study and other needs and expenses, so that the family can function well…."

Tiyasha is replying to my questions.

"And there's one more reason. After a conversation with my parents at that time, I felt that they did not consider my love for playing cricket seriously as they could not imagine that a girl could build up her career as a cricketer."

"Tiash, I feel it's not only with women cricket. It is the same for the boys. Some boys with not having a sound financial background also face similar situation.."

"Tell me, are you a right-handed or left-handed batsman?"

"I am both a lefty as a batsman and as a bowler."

"And …. Who is your favorite captain?"

"I have two favorites - Sourav Ganguly and Mithali Raj."

We, Tiyasha and me, met each other during our professional journey in 2009.

"Life never follows our wishes; we follow the wishes of life, Tiash", I say sadly.

"Why do you think so?"

"You are crazy about cricket. You did not get an opportunity for this. Life never follows your wishes."

"See, Anish, I love to play cricket. I saw a dream of becoming a cricketer for my team. Other required factors do not work for my passion. But I play cricket wherever I get an opportunity." she continues.

"And my love for this sport is alive in me. When I play, I absolutely enjoy this game. It's true that life does not follow my wishes, but is life able to put an end to my passion? I have the ability to moderate my life to go after my passion if I wish to do so."

Tiyasha's phone is ringing.

"Mom is calling. Let me talk to her, otherwise she will feel worried about me. You ask them about momos."

"Okay."

"How much time will it take to prepare our order?" I ask Sameer, one of the employees of this restaurant. He goes back to the kitchen of the restaurant to check and comes back to me.

"Mōmō tayārīki konta samayan padutundi.", (He says in his mother tongue 'Telegu' language, which means that some more time is required to prepare Momos.)

"Okay, I am standing out. Please call me when the food is

prepared."

I came out of the restaurant and check my phone. I need to call mom and Ananya. Mom had already called me twice, and my call log shows that Ananya had also called twice. I had missed their call. I often forget to change my mobile in general mode from silent mode, after coming back from the office.

We get sandwiched between our desires and other people's opinions. In some cases, we wish for something but it is not possible for us to execute it in our real life.

"When I get misguided between my wish and others' opinion regarding my wish, I look at the guiding star of my life. I interpret the direction of the guiding star of my life into words: I hear the words –

I am the captain of my life. I only understand myself better than anyone else. I need to ask myself four questions –

a) What is my desire?

b) Is fulfilling this desire really good for me, others, and humanity as a whole?

c) What is my attitude towards the execution of my desire?

d) How can I find a way to keep my ardor alive throughout my life?

We all have our own guiding star in our life. Respect and follow the guiding star."

Tiyasha told me about these at the beginning of the journey of our friendship.

THE CALMNESS OF LIFE

"Anish, what are you doing here?" I heard Tiyasha's voice. She came out.

"I'm going to call my elder child and the younger one. They've already called me twice. I missed it."

"You missed their call as you keep your phone on silent. Right?"

"Hmm."

Tiyasha smiles and says, "Call aunty." She goes inside the restaurant.

What should I say her? She knows my bad habit. They call her if I miss mom and Ananya's calls. Tiyasha either passes me the information or tries to fulfil their requirements for the reasons they called me.

To change my bad habit, she started to call me after I returned from office until I picked up her call.

Why does she call me? Only to remind me to change my call setting on my mobile from Silent to General or Vibrating Mode. At times, I miss her calls more than 22 to 30 times, but she never gives up.

"Yes, mom, tell me.", I call to my elder child.

"Anu called me. Today you go and pick her from the tuition class."

"Okay, Mom. I will go."

"She called me also."

"I know. You always missed our calls. For any type of emergency, I always call Tiyasha. It's no use calling you in this regard." I hear mom's angry tone.

"Hmmm. Okay."

I hung up the phone. I dial Ananya's number. She disconnects my call.

Mom calls Ananya as "Anu". When I hear this name, it stirs up an emotional storm inside me. Every time I try to tell to mom not to call Ananya by this name, Tiyasha does not make me do that. She says, "Anish, I know you are feeling pain. But by calling her Anu, she sees his son Anubhav in Ananya."

"You can adjust to your pain, but don't make her adjust to this pain because we don't all have the same ability to cope with our pains. And moreover, junior is also fine with the name. Let them be happy how they wish to become happy by coexisting peacefully with their scars."

I go and sit inside the restaurant.

"Where are the Momos?" I ask Tiyasha with irritation.

She sees my irritation and says, "It is still in the kitchen."

I look at her and understand that she is making fun of my anger.

"What happened? Did aunty scold you?"

"Yes. Mom's words make me aggravated sometimes. I know it is my bad habit to keep the phone in silent mode. I don't do it intentionally. I often forget it."

"Idigō mī mōmō", (Here is your Momo' in 'Telegu' language) Arun, one employee of this restaurant, tells Tiyasha.

"Now have Momos and cool down."

Arun serves food to us.

"Dhan'yavādālu", she says Thank you in Telegu to the guy.

"And I want to apologize. That time when I called you, I said many things, but I forgot to remind you regarding the settings of your phone. I am also one of the reasons for you getting a scolding from aunty." Tiyasha feels bad for his friend.

"Don't say sorry, yaar. I should think about this."

We started to eat our food.

"Why did they call you? Is everything fine?" Tiyasha asks.

"To pick up Ananya from her tuition class. Actually, Ananya had also called me, but I missed."

"Okay. I will also come with you."

I don't agree with Tiyasha's decision to come with me.

"You are already tired. Just go and have some sleep. And you only need to cook for yourself."

"No… just look at the time, it is already 8:12 pm. I will have this food now. That's sufficient. Today I did not get time to meet my junior. Let's finish it fast as we need to reach before time."

"Students need to be punctual, but it is not required for us, Tiash." I make fun of what she had just said.

" Elders need to be punctual first. Young learn from them."

Ananya and Tiyasha wait to meet each other. Today, Tiyasha

came late from the office. This is the only time they can meet each other. This is the reason I agree with my friend. We finish our food and leave for the tuition classes of my star.

"Let's go, junior." Tiyasha holds Ananya's hand.

Ananya was talking to her friends.

"Mani, how is your practice going?" she asks curiously.

"Good going, dear. Now, you tell me, how were your class-tests?"

"All were good, except mathematics. You know naa Mani, I am not good at it. "

"Did you have class-tests? You did not tell me anything in this regard?"

"Nish, I had class-tests. I prepared for the examination. Mani, my tutors and schoolteachers are there for me to help me with my studies. Didun is there to take care of me and you are there to take tension without any tension." she says and smiles at me.

"Tiash, are you listening to this girl?"

"She does not want to give you any stress. She knows very well what she needs to do." Tiyasha joins her junior. Now get ready to go to the house." Tiyasha checks the time and makes us aware that we need to get ready to go to our destination.

We reached our house. I dropped Ananya. Then I went to drop Tiyasha at her room.

Tiyasha stays in a rented room, near to my house. It takes hardly 30 minutes to walk there.

"You know, Tiash, when Ananya tells me, 'Nish, don't do it' or scolds me, I feel content. I feel life is pouring calmness on me.

I forget all the tiredness of life."

Tiyasha is listening and thinking in silence.

"What are you thinking, Tiash?"

"I am thinking of your feelings. It reminds me that some storms of life came and made me confused. Some storms messed up my life. Some storms tried to destroy me. I roamed here and there, overlooking my soul.

When I finally looked within my soul, I found one in a million who calms me down to discover the root causes of those storms. At that moment, I found the root cause and the storms of my life came to an end.

I now move with calmness in any of the haphazard situations of my life. The one in a million introduced me to the calmness in my life. She is the one for me, who emboldens me to create the new roadmap in the old life."

Tiyasha is a 'friend in need is a friend indeed.' As much as we have confusion, conflicts, and discordance, there is more concordance, reverence, and endearment in our friendship for each other.

"Anish, I don't know what the future holds for us, I believe that when we find the calmness in our lives, we will try to conquer all storms gracefully with the power of calm."

I remember the song, **"Andhakarer Pare"** (a song from the Bengali movie, "Ranjana Ami Ar Ashbona.").

One day, Ananya came to my room when I was listening to the song. She listened to the song and asked,

"Is this also one of your favorites, Nish?"

"Yes.", I replied to her.

"This is Mani's favorite also. She says that when she listens to the music, this song tells her that everywhere, in every situation, there is hope, but we should believe it from our heart."

"Do you believe this?"

"Yes, Didun every day takes medicine for her arthritis and does some light exercise as prescribed by her doctor.

She believes that she will be cured, that's why she regularly follows what the doctor said. That means she has genuine faith and hope inside her heart."

Each and every situation and understanding of them becomes more meaningful to us through music.

2019

LIFE IS CHEERFUL '.' or '?'

"Tiash", I went to her department.

She was busy signing some official documents. She did not hear me as she was completely lost in her work.

My phone is vibrating. I saw my boss number displayed on the screen.

"Hello, sir." I picked up the call.

"I am already in the office. Coming within five minutes." I informed him that I was in the office. I hung up the call.

"When did you come?" Tiyasha asked.

"Nearly fifteen minutes ago. You were busy signing those documents." I pointed towards the signed documents, which she had just completed.

"I needed to complete these before lunch. Sir will review these as tomorrow is the deadline for its submission."

"Why are you waiting? I did not even notice you. I just got stuck in finishing all this stuff."

"Today my team has a meeting with corporate quality assurance and research & development teams along with your team regarding the development of a new product at 4:30 pm."

"Yes, I remember. So, you need to extend your shift for this meeting."

"Of course. This meeting is very crucial for us."

"Yes, if we can manufacture this product with the desired quantity and quality, we will be able to meet the customer's requirement."

"And it will help in the advancement of our organization's business." I added my opinion.

"Tiash, I need the already submitted documents from you to review once before the meeting."

I am waiting for the documents. She is working upon the documents that I needed for the meeting.

"Take these and sign here." She told me.

I signed and received the documents and left her department.

It is 5:42 pm. We are at the end of our meeting. Tiyasha left the meeting as it was over for her team. Her team already had a discussion with other teams regarding their role in executing this new project in this meeting.

I am busy talking with our research and development team. Corporate quality assurance executives are reviewing the documents.

"Okay, so we can start the required process of manufacturing from next week." Ramesh, a team member of Research and Development, confirmed the starting timeline for this project.

"Okay we can start. We will try to procure some required resources within this week." I informed him.

"Done. Can we close the meeting?" He asked for approval from the other attendees who were present in this meeting room.

"Yes. We can." All approved for the closure of this meeting.

I always update my to-do list in the Google Keep Notes on my phone and on sticky notes on my laptop as it acts as a reminder for my activities to be completed. I was going to pick up my phone and laptop to update the details of the discussion from this meeting.

I took my phone and saw many missed calls from mom. I dialed her number and expected her scolding of high voltage.

"Hello, Babu." I heard her devastating tone.

"Mom, what happened?"

"Anu …." She was not able to finish her sentence.

"Mom, what happened to Dada? Mom, are you there?" I was not able to hear her voice and the call got disconnected.

My body was trembling. I was trying to control myself as I was at my office. I came out of the meeting room and went to the corridor.

I dialed mom again, but she was not picking up the call. I was trying to connect with her but I received a call from an unknown number.

"Hello.", I answered.

"Hi, this is Ramesh."

I made myself a quick shift from a broken personality to a cheerful one.

"Yaa, tell me.", I replied.

"Please update the minutes of the meeting and mail them."

"Sure." I disconnected the call.

I felt a hand on my shoulder.

"Anish.", Tiyasha called me.

"You come with me to the cafeteria." She takes me to our cafeteria.

"You have to go to Hyderabad as soon as possible. Anu Da is no more." Tiyasha says in a shaking voice. Elder brother in Bengali is called "Dada" or sometimes when the person is addressed by his name, 'Da' is added to show respect. .)

I am Anish Mukherjee, who again became alone without my second umbrella, after my father.

"When and how?" I fumble.

"Today afternoon, around 3o'clock. His car got crashed by a truck in a road accident. One of his colleagues informed Manan. He only told Aunty."

Manan is an employee of our bookstore.

"Tiash, Ramesh needs me to send the updates on the minutes of the meeting. The upcoming project for us will be postponed without sharing these details. I'm not able to understand what I should do."

" How much time is required to compile the details from you?"

"Maximum 15-20 minutes."

"Give it to me. I will prepare and send it to you. You can review them and send it to him."

We sat in the cafeteria. She collected all the details from me and helped me, like a father or mother helps to organize all the required things for a disorganized son, a sister or brother cooperates with an unsystematic brother to show the way to get the things done systematically. That day, I felt she was not only my friend, she was the direction of a person when the person loses control over himself.

"I am booking your flight tickets. Go to your work desk and complete all the formalities for your early leave."

"Yup." I left for my department.

"We are like the live performing artist in the stage of our profession. A live performing artist makes us happy without expressing his personal happiness or sadness to us. He performs and makes us understand through the walks of his life that life is cheerful irrespective of the situation." she said after some days. I saw the pain and respect in her eyes that day for the artists who perform live on stage.

Is life really cheerful? Or Life is cheerful – what is the truth of life? We always get sandwiched between "? (Question mark)" and ". (Full stop)" to understand it.

CERTAINTY OF UNCERTAINTY

"Tell me, Tiash."

"Check your office mail. I have already sent it."

"I will."

I disconnected the call and opened my office mail. I reviewed the details of the meeting.

Finally, I sent the details of the meeting to Ramesh for the upcoming project of our organization.

Tiyasha booked evening flight tickets for me. My flight was at 8:40 pm.

"Tiash…What will I do now? I am not able to move my body. I have no energy left inside of me.", I broke down in tears, sitting in a cab, heading towards the airport.

"Are you okay, sir?" The cab driver asked me.

"I am okay, bhaiya." I told him with a forced smile.

"Anish, no one is there for Aunty and your star except you. You have to stay strong. You don't have any other option." I heard Tiyasha's consoling words.

"Hmmm." I was trying to control my tears.

"Hmm… will you come with me, Tiash?" I was scared to go there. Finally, I asked my friend as I really felt to have her with me.

"Anish, I can come with you. But I should stay with Aunty and Ananya. Tell me, who will stay with them? You are strong, dear. You have to go alone."

"Hmm. At least you stay with them. I am at least relaxed that you are there with them. I'll try to manage myself."

I directly reached the airport from the office and informed Manan. He asked me to come home once. I denied coming and told that I would not have enough time for boarding. Actually, I was not able to face Ananya and Mom.

My plane took off. I saw the darkness in the sky at night, and it gave me a feeling that this darkness was engulfing my life. I closed my eyes and saw Dada in front of me.

"Why are you sleeping?" Dada asked me.

"I am tired, Dada."

"My bro, we are the riding horses of our family. I was born for short race and you are born for the long race. Ani, the horse never rest. He is always ready for any situations. He rests so that he can run faster than before."

I woke up with full of tears in my eyes. I felt like calling Tiyasha, but I was in the plane. I checked my phone. Many messages were piled up as unread messages in the inbox. I was not feeling well to read them.

I don't know how Mom is? How is Ananya? Will she understand? Should I tell her? Did anyone say anything to her?

I was scrolling down my phone screen and saw the missed message from my dear friend.

"Anish, I can feel your pain, but I cannot take away your pain. You know, I trust the power of my belief towards the sun of my soul whenever I go through the dark phase of my life.

The sun always rises and guides us to find the way so that we can shine and help others to shine in their journey of life.

The rising of the sun is the symbol of certainty, but we ourselves are uncertain. We need to discover some certainty, even in midst of uncertainty. Through our efforts, we can attempt to convert some uncertainty into certainty.

I never look back; I always try to look forward. Do you know why?

When I look forward, I stand and see only the sun of my soul in front of me; she is the tunes of my life.

I am sure, dear, you also have the sun of your soul in your life. Find the sun and search for something certain left in the midst of uncertainty. This certainty of uncertainty will help you move forward wholeheartedly.

Take care, my friend."

I received the message from her at 8:15 pm. I did not wish to check my mobile. I remembered that she starts her morning with the song **"Tor jonyo sokal bhangche"** (a song from the Bengali movie "Antaraal".)

Whatever the situations are, at least someone's genuine care and his or her effort to connect himself or herself with your pain, makes you feel like someone giving you water after walking so many miles in a very hot climate without food, water, rest, or umbrella.

INVISIBLE THREADS OF CONNECTION

Anubhav Das was an IT Project Manager and worked in Hyderabad. He was my elder brother by heart and not by birth.

Anubhav came to Vizag from Orissa for his job. We have our own house in Vizag. He took the first floor of our house on rent. He was raised by his uncle and his uncle's family. He was very young when he lost both his parents. His uncle stayed in Orissa with his own family.

I remember that I was in Class IX when he started to live in our house. Dada used to come to me and enquire about my studies. After returning from the company, he came to our room to teach me. He helped me complete my homework. Gradually, he became like my elder brother and I became his 'Babu', He loved me as his brother, friend, and son.

Dada performed all duties and responsibilities as if he was the son of this family. We have a small book store, "Aasaan". Dad decided its name. He runs the book store. My mom was a primary school teacher in Vizag. I lost my father during my early college days.

Dada never made me feel like my father was not in this world. He became my father through all these tough days. I never faced the struggle a son feels without his dad. He took care of mom. He did not allow Mom to leave her job after Dad's death.

"Anu, I need to quit the job, otherwise our bookstore will start incurring loss. I will be able to not accept that as it is your uncle's heart. He loved this store as much as he loved his family."

"Mom, who says that Uncle's love will become ignorant for us? Let me think. But please don't quit the job for the sake of this. Women always sacrifice for others' sake; I think that they should not do that. We, as men should also sacrifice if the situation demands."

Dada addressed my father as 'Uncle' but called my mother as 'Mom.'

"Dada, why do you address them like this?"

"I don't know why I address them like this. But it's what I feel from my heart."

He recruited many people for our book store for its smooth functioning. Our small business started flourishing and improved our family's financial condition.

My flight landed. I came out of the airport. I checked the time. It is 10:04 pm.

I called up Rahul Bhatia, one of Dada's colleagues.

"Hello, Anish."

"Hi, I have landed. Where do I need to go?"

" You better wait there. I am coming to receive you. You stay tonight in my room."

"No. I can find a cab and a hotel for myself. You tell me the place. I will search for it."

"Anish, I am like your elder brother. So please just listen to me. You are new here. I am coming to receive you."

I am waiting at airport.

"Hello. Have you reached?" Tiyasha called me.

"Hmm…. Yes…. Where are you?"

"At your house, Anish."

"Okay. Mom and Ananya – what are they doing?"

"Aunty is not having food. She is hiding her tears in front of your star."

"And…I don't know whether she understood or not, but she is behaving normally. She came to aunty and told her not to cry and hugged her."

"Hmmmm. There may be a chance that she is thinking that dada will call at night, as he did when he had some important meetings."

"May be. We need to observe her. You just complete all the required formalities over there and come back. We will discuss about her."

"Tiash, do you remember Rahul, one of dada's friends?"

"No re. I don't remember. But what happened?"

"He is coming to receive me and I'll stay at his room tonight."

"Okay. It's fine. Please have dinner yaar."

"Hmm. And I want to thank you for your message. I missed the message as I was not feeling well to check my phone. I felt that if the sun of your soul would ever know your love and respect towards her and how much she becomes your strength, I hope she would feel good to know these."

"Hmm… but the real love, respect, and belief towards a

person always remains there inside your, which is reflected through both your words and actions."

"Had your dinner?"

"No. Ruma, Aunty, Junior and I—we will have dinner together. She may or may not be aware of this news. I feel that she knew it, but she tried not to show this to anyone."

I felt worried. "Did Ananya ask anyone about her dad?"

"She asked Ruma, but Ruma did not say anything. She hid the news from our star by pretending that she needs to complete the household work quickly."

"Why do you think so?"

"She made a sketch of a man who looks like Anu Da and a little girl who was waving her hand to him from a balcony. I felt that she had drawn herself." I heard Tiyasha's cry for the first time from the time she heard the news.

Tiyasha completed the description of the sketch by saying, "The man was waving his hand to the little girl from the clouds in the sky",

"She was lost in her sketching." Tiyasha controlled her tears.

"I also felt that she understood about her dad."

"Tiash, I feel a scream in my heart. I am not able to imagine that I will not see dada in person. I will not cuddle dada. He will not speak to me ever again. I will not receive any hug or punch. I will never hear his scolding again. I will never feel relaxed that dada is there for me."

Tiyasha was silent on the other end of the call.

"Anish, from the time I received a call from Aunty, sometimes I feel like lumps in the throat and heaviness in the chest."

"I am remembering the person who always becomes a catalyst for me to fight with the emotional battles of my life and makes me robust to help others in their hard times."

Tiyasha always remembers who stays with her soul in each known and unknown moment of life. The person never connects with Tiyasha by the definition of relationship but is connected through God's invisible threads of connection.

This is the connection where any condition is not able to beat unconditional, where no expectation beats expectation. Here humanity and true emotions of a life win and become a vigor for a person in the rain or shine of his or her life.

Tiyasha listens to the song **"Bolte chai na"** (song from a Bengali short film "Rannaburi."). Today I also feel like listening this song. I play the music on my mobile and close my eyes.

Music is a healer, as we all know, but those who are working hard to heal us through music, will never understand them or their hard work if we see it only with our eyes or if we hear it only through our ears. Tiyasha always tries to understand and respect their diligence to keep us well in the excruciating days of our life.

SIMPLE ANGLES OF TANGLES

Rahul came to receive me and we went to his home. He told me to take rest but I stayed over there with restlessness.

I was not able to call Mom. I feel a fear inside me that she will understand that I am crying. It would make them feel the emptiness created by the death of dada. I did not want to do this. Tiyasha and Ruma were there with her. Dada became a support system for her and, obviously, for our family.

Memories were becoming unbound, as well as my tears.

I got my first job in Sikkim in 2009, after completing my graduation in Mechanical Engineering. That day, I saw tears of joy in his eyes. I felt that I was seeing my dad in him. He hugged me tightly. That day, my inner voice echoed, "Your success is his success, your happiness is his happiness, your sadness is his sadness."

I reminisce about that day's conversation when I got a new job in the "City of Destiny". Tiyasha came from Sikkim to Vizag in 2016. We are destined to be together to pursue our professional journey along with our amity.

"Why is the name "Aasaan" for the bookstore?" Tiyasha asked.

"Don't know." I answered.

"A book teaches us, educates us, shows us the right path, and motivates us. The combination of teaching, education, showing us the right direction, and motivation makes our lives easy. Uncle might have thought it in this manner. ."

"A chain of thought behind the name!" I exclaimed.

Dada was doing some work in his notebook.

"The name was decided by my uncle and got its actual meaning in reality mainly due to Anu Da. His efforts for this store make many lives "Aasaan" ('easy' in Hindi)."

Dada smiled at her and again got busy with his work. I agreed with her words.

Dada never thought about the relationship he has with us. He met us, associated with us, and built his own family. When I see Tiyasha, I find some traits of dada in her. Wherever she goes, she builds a profound connection with the surroundings.

Tiyasha and dada are very close to each other. Tiyasha grew up as a single child. I noticed that people came and shared their inner pain and problems with my friend, but who was there for her?

"Anish, I never thought about this. I feel happy to walk alone." She gracefully smiled, "I have a sun within my soul, who shows me the way to rise alone, shine, and make others glow with the rays of shining without any expectations. This way of direction helps me to understand the simple angles of the tangles of a life."

Dada always said, Yes, Tiyasha was a true blue to the songbird of her life in any situation. The songs of the songbird are the powerful melodious contributors to spreading positivity in our lives and in our society, amidst much surrounding negativity.

ETERNAL RESPECT

I heard from Manan that dada also became a helping hand for him and the employees of the store so that they could earn money independently through their hard work in an honest way.

The majority of this store's employees were previously unemployed due to a lack of basic education and who did not have enough money to complete their education. Some middle-aged people, who need to earn money for their family but are not able to do physical heavy labor due to their health problems are recruited by dada for our book store.

Manan's sister Ruma stays most of the time with mom, and is a helping hand for our work. This way at least, she will be able to complete her basic education. So Dada told Mom to teach her as well.

"I denied taking Sir's help as I knew that he wanted to help us in some way. I only have my mom and sister in my family."

"Manan, mom is getting older day by day. School and household work is becoming difficult for her to manage. She needs a helping hand for herself. Ruma will assist her and mom will teach her as well. Education is important to her. Once she completes her education, she can get a job and help you and your mom." Dada tried to convince him.

When uncle, that is, Tiyasha's father, came to Vizag to stay with his daughter, he spent most of his time sitting, reading and buying books from our store. In their free time, Dada and Tiyasha taught uncle to use computers and digital platforms. Middle-aged employees of our store got benefits from uncle's learning as he taught them. Overall, it helped us to grow our business with this e-learning of our older generations. But it created problems for Aunty, Tiyasha's mother. Uncle got busy with the computer when he stayed in his home town and spent less time with aunty. Uncle's teachers – both my dada and my friend got scolded from aunty for this.

I laughed alone in the silent dark room of Rahul while walking through the lanes of memory.

I remembered the heart-touching song **"Jodi aar ektu somoy dite"**, the song from the Bengali movie "Bheetu", which is a favorite of all three of us. I played the song on my mobile. I once heard this song with Tiyasha and this song made our emotions flow in the form of tear drops.

But today, I was not able to hold my tears as the song became the most significant in my life for my dada. But this song still remains a favorite for the three of us, although Dada is no more with us.

"When the sun rises, I wake up with her song. When the moon comes to light up the sky at night, I listen to her music. When the earth brings different seasons in our life as well as in the nature of our earth, I listen to her songs every seasons." Tiyasha always expressed her feelings when she talked about her favorite singer.

The presence or absence of a music listener never puts an end to his respect for a song and a singer. It remains in the memory of his near and dear ones after his death also. He has an everlasting respect for his favorite singer and song beyond any condition.

COACHES OF OUR LIFE

I was remembering the old days of brotherhood.

I had recently joined a new organization in Sikkim. I was partying with my colleagues on December 31st, 2009.

We, all boys, met together for a celebration of the New Year party. After party we slept in Harish's room, one of my team mates.

In the morning, I jolted from my sleep due to dada's call.

"Where are you?" I heard his polite but firm voice.

"At Harish's room."

"What happened yesterday? Why did you not call your mom? She called you more than 30 times. Tiyasha sent a text to you and informed the same." He asked me.

"Dada, I came for the celebration of the New Year to his room. Everything is fine. No need for mom to worry. "

"It is fine, I understand. You can call your mom to say the same thing that you said to me now. When she hears your voice, she would be assured that her son is fine and would be less worried."

"Dada, only one day, I did not call her.", I felt agitated by his words.

He felt that agitation in my voice.

"You did not do the right thing. We are not so busy that we are not able to connect to our loved ones. Mom was busy in her personal and professional life, but she still called you. She never forgot her duty for a single day, but you forgot."

"I am not like mom or like you." I argued with him and disconnected the call without giving him an opportunity to say anything to me. I got very irritated as I felt that every day I called her, what could happen if I didn't call her one day.

"Anish, I also texted you right to just call aunty once." we sat in a restaurant in Sikkim and discussed the same with Tiyasha.

"I thought of calling you to inform mom that I am busy with my colleagues."

"Anish, hearing your voice is a consolation for mom that her son is fine, when you are far from her. I can inform aunty, but it will not make her relaxed which hearing from you can do.", Tiyasha also disagreed with me.

I got irritated with her just way as I was with dada.

"Sometimes you inform mom. Right?" I asked her with annoyance.

"Yes, I do it, but only when there's an emergency or sometimes when you are really unable to take her call. But, my friend, were you really not able to call aunty once on the 31st night? You forgot, that is okay for me. After seeing my text also, you did not think to call her once."

"Tiash, dada loves me but, that day, dada scolded me badly. You are also saying this all. Only mom did not say anything to me."

"Now that you have said the truth, why aunty should be placed on top above everything and everyone. She was worried, but never had any complaint against you. Dada scolded you so that you won't repeat the same and make mom feel worried. I am not supporting you for the same reason as dada." She tried to make me understand the reality which I was not able to understand.

I talked for a very short time with dada and Tiyasha after this discussion, but they behaved how they had always treated me with love, affection, and care.

Later, I realized that I was wrong when I was not able to talk to mom for almost one and a half day. I realized the pain of staying far from my mom and my loved ones without talking to them for even a single day.

'I believe that 'our well wishers will never hurt us and will always say lofty words' – is a myth. The real well wishers will say some harsh truths, which can break our heart. They will scold you if you make a mistake, but they will also try to find a way for you to correct your mistake.

After everything, they still want you hold your racket again to play the ping-pong ball of life, freely and decisively. They will not control you or your decision, but they will strongly advise you to be cautious.

Well-wishers are our life coaches. We are the players of our life." Tiyasha said this after two years, when I realized my mistake.

FOLLOWERS, CREATORS AND MODERATORS

My phone rang and Tiyasha's number was on display.

"Hello," I said.

" Did you have your dinner?"

"I had 'Puli hora' with curd."

'Puli hora' is a popular South-Indian dish.

"Now try to get some sleep, Anish."

"Sleep has eluded me but many thoughts are flowing in my heart." I said dejectedly," I will not be able to cope with the loss of my brother."

We both were carefully and patiently listening to each other.

"I informed the office regarding this mishap. Where is Ananya?"

" Just look at the time. She is already in deep sleep."

"Tiash, do you remember the days when star came to our house for the first time?"

"Yes, she was probably three to four years old."

"And do you remember that day when Anu da gave his

decision to Aunty for the first time?"

"She tried to call me …..."

"But she was unable to reach you due to network issues." Tiyasha completed my sentence.

"Yes. When she finally connected with me, I bore the brunt of her anger. I was so puzzled about what to I say that time. That was another reason for her to get more irritated. How could I say anything as I was not aware of anything? Dada did not discuss it with me or anyone else. He only told Mom that time."

"Yes, but when Aunty started to take care of Ananya, her own thought and emotions changed towards the little girl. Our little star used to get irritated when aunty instructed Ruma to take care of our star, and went to the kitchen to bring food for her."

"Ananya spends very little time away from her grandmother. She has a genuine concern for mom at this young age."

"Hmmm.", I heard a sigh from Tiyasha.

"I don't know how I will face her. How will she face this phase of her life? How could I manage anything without dada?" I felt an unbearable pain for my star and me.

Dada adopted Ananya. We, Tiyasha and me, supported his decision and we were both very happy with it. Dada's friends, Tiyasha's parents, and some of our friends were also there to support him wholeheartedly. Mom initially halfheartedly supported his decision but she eventually supported him in all formalities as she was a mom. Now she is the one who loves her grand-daughter more than anyone of us, and we get scolding for scolding her grand-daughter. Dada was a single father. Ananya is the single daughter of Dada and a single child cum leader of the future generation of our family.

I checked the time. It was 2:00 am.

"Anu Da is there with you all the time. He is in your heart, so why to search for him outside? Anish, people who love you genuinely and unconditionally wish well for you, they always walk with your soul."

" Go off to sleep. You have your office tomorrow, Tiash. ."

I hung up the call. I got up from the bed, stood in front of the window of Rahul's room. I look at the starry sky. I heard the inner words of my soul and which said that dada became a big star in the sky, but he left Ananya, my little star, on this earth.

Suddenly, I saw a glimmer of hope. This light guided the wanderer in me to complete my duty and dada's unfinished works.

Tiyasha was right, I needed to look deep within myself.

We should not be the blind followers of any rules or regulations in our lives. We need to moderate them to make good things happen to us and others. We are the followers, creators, and moderators of the principles of our own life based on our needs and situations.

SHELTER OF A STORMY LIFE

"Good morning." Rahul woke me up.

"Hey, good morning." I replied.

"You get freshened up and come for breakfast." he tells me.

I checked my phone and saw a missed call from my mom. I called her.

"Babu, are you fine?"

"Yes, mom. I am okay."

"I will go with a friend of dada to complete the required formalities. You take care of yourself, mom."

"When will you complete all formalities?"

"I don't know exactly how much time it will take to complete. Let's see. Where is Ananya?"

"Anu is here only."

I was severely shocked by her words, and some unpleasant thoughts were coming to mind -

How is mom? What's her reaction as Anu is with her.

"What are you saying, mom? How dada would be with you now over there?"

"She is here only."

She started to call Ananya 'Anu' from the day, dada left us. Earlier mom called our star 'Niya'.

However, I was somewhat relaxed by understanding her.

"Okay, Mom. I will see you soon. Take care."

I went for breakfast. Rahul had taken this house on rent. It is a nice and well decorated house.

"Have it," Rahul said, handing me an idly with chutney and sambar, along with his plate of breakfast.

"Anish, take care of yourself first. You need to stay strong."

"Hmm…. Thank you for your help and concern for me."

Rahul stays alone in this house. His parents, who were in Ahmedabad, often came to stay with him.

We finished our breakfast and went to complete all formalities. He and other friends of dada helped me. Most of the formalities were completed by evening.

Rahul came to the airport to drop me as I had my flight from Hyderabad at 10:20 pm. Tiyasha booked the flight for me. Rahul assured me that he would follow-up to complete the pending formalities as soon as possible. I might have to come again if needed. He hugged me and assured me that he would be there for me anytime.

I thanked him. I feel blessed that I met him during the toughest periods of my life. We bid good bye to each other and I went inside the airport.

I completed my security check and was waiting for the boarding call.

I opened Google Keep notes on my phone. I started to

update the upcoming projects and listen the song "**Ekla Anek Door**" (from the Bengali Movie "Ranjana Ami Ar Ashbona").

When I listen this song, I always remember my friend as she tries to follow this song and implement the significance of it in her life as per her own thought process. She always said, "This song brings out the message for me that I can fight alone to achieve my dreams and to complete my responsibilities towards me, my loved ones and, other people even if the situation creates any obstacles."

Tiyasha always updates her upcoming projects. She updates

- 1) What was the life lesson from that day?

- 2) How much of this learning is required to be implemented in her life?

- 3) How much of this learning is actually required for the sake of one's life?

She updates the answers to these three questions daily at the end of each day.

My today's updates are -

1. I will raise Ananya in the proper way with the help of Mom, Dada's thoughts and my friend Tiyasha.

2. I will take care of my mom.

3. I will take care of our book store and my professional life.

4. I will take care of Tiyasha and our amity.

5. I will take …

I heard boarding call for my flight. I stopped updating my Google Keep notes, closed it and started heading for the aircraft.

My plane took off. I am going to Vizag with lots of responsibilities and wishes. **"Chalo jai"**, a song from the Bengali movie "Ranjana Ami Ar Ashbona", is playing on my mobile.

"I respect her, not only for entertaining us, but most significantly, on my toughest days, I take shelter under the umbrella of her song. She is the shelter for me in the thunderstorm of my life." Tiyasha said while talking about the sun of her soul.

Musicians and their creations bring sunny days to the rainy season of our lives.

Plants of the past become trees of the present with the soil of love, care, respect, affection, water of knowledge and experience, lights of understanding and winds of hope.

2022

SEARCHLIGHT OF A SAILOR

We sit on the Rk Beach, that is, Ramakrishna Beach. It is a very famous beach and tourist spot. It got its name due to its proximity to Ramakrishna Mission ashram

Today I had the morning shift. Tiyasha left early and went to my house. Mom came with us and we picked up Ananya from her school.

Almost two hours have passed since I came here. I am narrating the past waves of our life to myself in front of the waves of the sea while listening to the song "**Amader Kothagulo**", from the Bengali movie "Chini".

Waves come and go back to their origins. Sometimes they touch us, and sometimes they snatch our lives. They flow according to their desires, and we act as observers.

I sit on the seaside. Tiyasha, Mom and my Star went to visit Ramakrishna Mission Ashram.

We try to avoid the places with heavy rush in the utmost possible way. At the same time, I feel good to see that the tourists are visiting the tourist spots in our country.

Due to COVID 19, tourism industry suffered very badly. But now it is gradually reviving to its normal.

People all around the world have faced financial instability due to COVID. We have seen a gradual improvement in our country and the world's economy since the first wave of COVID-19.

"You have suppressed the pain inside you for the sake of Ananya and aunty. But every year, this day, you just want to escape from them. For the first time, you are not able to escape the day." Tiyasha said to me in the office cafeteria today.

"Just tell me, how could I deny? Star is growing up. She now understands everything. She requested me that we all go somewhere today after her school."

"She understands you, Anish, and also your grief."

"Hmm. I feel a numbness inside me on this day, Tiash, all the memories flash across my mind about how we spent those days."

We both sit silently. Both we have gone through the uphill of our lives. We shared our thoughts with each other, but we never shared them with anyone. We take care of each other and the loved ones of each other. We connect our lives with music, with the unconditional principles of humanity. We listen to each other's words. We are connected via the shadows of our friendship.

"I was thinking of the days when no one was there with me, but just a person," Tiyasha was saying.

I interrupted her.

"But a person, whom you listened through the waves of sound from many miles. And even now you listen to her songs, but digitally.", I completed her sentence.

I know her devotion towards that person.

"And whose songs become the searchlight of a sailor of a ship of a life. She is my ideal."

"She lights up the moments of people's lives through her songs, without letting her audience know about her personal struggles, happiness, or sadness. I learned the morals of many episodes of life from her." I heard the language of her emotions.

FOOTPRINTS OF BLUEPRINTS

We are in our house now, and Tiyasha is in her room.

"Ananya showed me her sketch, the one she made on the day of Anu da's death and said …" Tiyasha told me when we were sitting on the beach. Ananya and mom went to buy some handicrafts, sold by an old person on the side of the beach.

"Oh. You didn't tell me about it that day," I interrupted her.

"Yes, because you were worried whether she knew the news of her dad's death or not. So, I just told you that she made a sketch."

"Hmmm, what did she say?"

"She had told me that dad is always there behind the cloud. He is looking at us from the cloud, Mani."

I felt tears in my eyes. I stared at Tiyasha as she paused. I saw her teary eyes.

"That means she heard about the death." I asked Tiyasha.

"She told me that she heard the conversation between Ruma and aunty."

"How could she be so normal when even I could not be?"

"She was not normal. She behaved normally in front of us."

I felt the pain through Tiyasha's words.

"Ananya said that dad will never come to meet us. But he will be there behind the clouds. I hugged my junior and she hugged me tightly. She was crying. She was waiting for someone with whom she could share her anguish. We were hiding this news from her and acting like nothing had happened. We were wiping our tears and became silent when she came to us."

"Hmmmm... what could we do, Tiash?"

"I feel at least we should go and talk to her to understand her feelings and pain. Did she understand the depth of the news and how much did she understand. Although she might not understand many things in reality, but she still has her own perception.. She can imagine many things, but she still connects them to the real world through her own thought process. We should act on the basis of her understanding, "

"Tiash, you already knew my condition." I said helplessly.

"Hey, don't feel bad, I also needed to think this way. I understood that after many hours of that day."

"Tiash, thanks yaar for everything."

"Not accepted."

"Yes, I knew your answer."

We are watching the night view of the beach. Our friendship started in the mountainous terrain. This friendship made its own way, and now we are on a tour of this port city.

Tiyasha always tries to learn something new. She learns different regional languages of our country along with international languages. She listens to the songs in different language. She watches movies and theatres in different languages. She spends her free time by sitting at the book store, reading and buying books.

When we travel by any vehicle or we are on a road trip, we take a halt to eat food, she loves to hear the stories of the lives of the drivers or the people who serve us. I have seen that they also love to share their stories with her. She buys books from hucksters when she travels by train. She talks with them and listens to them until the next station or her destination.

You will always see my friend, every time with one constant thing, that is music. She leads her life with the rhythms of music. She leads her life with the lyrics of the music. She leads her life by sharing songs with her loved ones. She tries to keep all of us connected with music. When we get frustrated, we start to fight or argue, she plays the music and we start to discuss the argument or fight.

I have seen my friend very closely; I have seen many people come and go from her life. She meets them and greets them while they come, stay, and leave. She adores both the bitter and sweet flavors of her life.

Among them, there is a person who will never know that Tiyasha Roy walks each step of all aspects of life with the music. The musical footprints of the person create the blueprints of Tiyasha's life.

Mom entered my room and said, "Babu…"My thoughts' threads lead me from my dear friend to my dear mother.

"Yes, mom. Why are you still awake?"

"Watching a television serial. Today's episode is very interesting."

"Okay. Let's finish watching and come here."

"I came in the middle of the advertisement."

"Okay. What were you saying?"

"After so many years, today I felt happy on this day. My elder Anu takes care of me the same way little Anu feels for me. She gave me a sketch today."

"Okay. Show me."

Mom went to bring the sketch. I am happy to see mom and hear her words. Seeing her happy, I am happy.

"See this."

I saw the sketch of a girl feeding a lady and a person's photo in front of them. I feel that the girl is Ananya. She sketched herself. The lady is her grandmother, and the photo of the person is her dad.

I don't have any words to say to mom. I hug the paper sketch. I feel that I will cry, but don't want to do it in front of mom.

"The thought behind the sketch is very nice, mom."

"Yes. She wants to take care of me in this way. Does she want to say this through her sketch, Babu?"

"Did you not ask her?"

"No. Why do I need to ask her? I understood. The advertisement is about to end. The serial will start again. You go off to sleep."

"Hmm."

I remembered Tiyasha's words.

"Tiash, you know, drawing teacher said that my star is doing well in sketching" I told her proudly.

"She loves to do this. She expresses her silent words through her passion."

It is 10:56 pm.

I dialed Tiyasha's number.

"Hello" She picked up my call.

"Are you sleeping?"

"Not exactly. Writing something."

I hear the song "**Dhulomakha Canvas**" from a Bengali movie 'Sesh Sangbad', from the background. Tiyasha plays the songs after dinner and always writes something before going to sleep.

"Tiash, did Ananya show you any sketch that she made today?"

"Yes. She showed it to me before going to practice cricket."

"I saw the sketch now and felt tears in my eyes."

"Anish, this is Ananya's birthday gift to her dad. She made it for her grandmother on her dad's birthday."

RESPECT OF THE UNIVERSE

"Tiash, how could you say that she is the best person in this world for you?"

"She is the person who sows the seeds of those qualities that build me from 'Yesterday's me' to 'Today's better me'.

She uplifts me to concentrate on myself first. She indoctrinates me to think about myself, and when I start to think, I start introspection.

This introspection clears the lens of my mind. I get a clear vision of areas of my improvement in every aspect of my life.

She moves me towards my growth gradually from "Today's better me" to "Tomorrow's best me".

The person who paves the way for me to achieve the best version of myself every day, slowly but steadily, she is the best person in this world for me."

"That means we all have a best person in the world for us."

"Yes, you need to understand that. First you think, who is the best person in the world for you?"

We are sitting on Rk beach and its 6:54 in the evening. I am feeling comforted by the evening's breeze from the beach. Tiyasha directly came to the beach from her office. She had the morning shift and I have the night shift. I am thinking the answer to her question.

"Tiash, Ananya..." I almost shout, seeing Tiyasha listening to the song "**Mithye Premer Gaan**", song from a Bengali web-series, "Break-up story."

She was startled by my shout.

"Where?"

"Duffer, Ananya is the best person in the world for me."

"Oh... okay." Tiyasha smiles, and her smile says to me that she knew my answer. How could that be?

"Hey, why are you smiling? Did you know my answer?"

"Yes. A friend has an extra ear to listen to a friend's silent words."

I laughed. It is absolutely true; she understands me better than any of my friends. Today we visited Kalimata Temple, situated near Rk, the beach of the 'Jewel of East Coast", just before coming to the beach.

"Tiash, what did you pray to Kali Maa?"

"I would not tell this to you or anyone what I prayed for."

"Okay, madam."

"Time flies, I adjust the velocity of leading my life with respect to the velocity of time. I try to adjust my speed of running in the world of rat race. Sometime I win, sometimes I lose as per the rules of any race.

Before everything, I feel that I have a duty to the person and to her well-being, who enriches my life along with my parents, my teachers, and my friends through her song. She is the song of new leaves in the season of my life's falling leaves. She is the best person in the world for me."

"What is the duty?"

"Creators felicitate us through their medium of creativity, through their devotion. We can't do anything for them, but we can pray every day for them in our own way, we can wish well for them so that they stay well, healthy and can prosper in their personal and professional lives, we can send our love and respect towards them to the Universe."

I captured Tiyasha's handwritten birthday wish note to the person who is the best person in the world for my friend,

"You help us to celebrate our moments of life with your music. You change our mood with your song. With your words, you modify our perspective on life. You guide us to live with hope. You teach us how to love ourselves first and how to love and respect others.

For me, every day is your birthday as your music makes us happy for many more 364 days, many more 24 hours, many more 60 minutes, many more 60 seconds of our life.

 Sound and silence;

Chaos and calmness;

Every time, everywhere, you are the respect of the Universe."

SUN OF THE SOULS

"It's encouraging to see that interest in women's cricket in India is growing among young girls these days. What about the parents? Will they encourage their daughters? – What do you think?" Shravan, one of our friends, asked Tiyasha.

Tiyasha, Shravan, Divya and me - we, four work mates get together at Divya's house after office as we had general shifts. Mahesh, Divya's husband also joins us. We are having pizza-pasta party. Ananya and Shravya, Divya's daughter, are also enjoying themselves.

"It depends on the thought process of each of them. The financial condition of the family is also one prime factor which cannot be ignored. I personally feel that a girl or boy who is interested in cricket or in any other sports, needs to complete their basic education. Education develops humans in all aspects of their life towards the right direction"

"And humans build up one society. Education develops humans and humans develop society." I say having a bite of pizza.

Today is Women's Day. Our office organized a women's cricket tournament among their female employees. Tiyasha and Divya, two women from the same department, were opponents in the tournament. Divya is a team member of the champion team. Tiyasha's team finished this tournament in third position. My friend Tiyasha Roy was awarded as the woman of the tournament.

We were all talking but I saw Tiyasha's tacit.

"What happened? Why have you turned to as a person without noise?" I make fun of her.

"No, I am thinking about Anushka."

" Do you remember the tug of war game organized by our office in 2019? How well she played.", Divya queried.

"Cinnā ('small' in Telegu) was a very jolly girl. I remember those days."

We used to call Anushka 'Cinnā'. She was very hard-working and extremely close to Tiyasha's heart.

"I never believed it when I heard the news." Tiyasha remembered the day when we came to know that Anushka had died due to Covid 19 in the first wave of 2020.

" Every day, I see her face in front of me, Divya. How she smiled, how she worked with us, how she made fun of me."

"You loved her neat and clean work style. You appreciated her work all the time." Divya narrated the past in a way that made her feel like those days reeling in front of her that moment.

I saw the tears for their colleague.

Time passes, people remain. No one is lost because they become the pages of our memory book.

"Nish, let's go. Mani is already tired today. She needs proper rest."

"Tiyasha, she is very caring towards you." Divya praises my star.

"Yes, she is. She cares for me, cares for Anish, cares for aunty, cares for everyone." Tiyasha also appreciates Ananya.

"She cares for me also, Aunty." Shravya says, sitting beside her mom.

Shravya and Ananya are schoolmates but Shravya is younger than my Star.

"Anish, let's go." Tiyasha asks me.

We hail an auto from the bus stop near Divya's house. We reached our bus stop within 45 minutes of leaving.

"Mani, Tata. See you tomorrow." She waves her hand.

"Good night junior."

"Can you go?"

"Yes, sir."

"Have your medicine before you go off to sleep, madam."

"Okay. Good night."

Since the death of Anushka, I have seen Tiyasha remain silent for many months.

We see a person in front of us regularly and we work with them every day. They share their problems with us and we share ours with them. We consider them as colleagues, but they become a part of our life.

"Mom, we lost the match and I got awarded the women of the tournament's prize." Tiyasha said to Aunty.

I was standing beside her, seeing her face glowing with happiness. This happiness reflected the happiness of her soul.

Tiyasha finished talking with Aunty.

"What did aunty say?" I asked my friend.

"She was very happy but worried for me if I got injured. I assured her that I was absolutely fine."

"Okay. What else?" I wanted to hear her words of happiness.

"I dedicate these happy moments to my parents and to the best person in the world for me."

"Parents will know about your happiness. How will your best person know that you dedicated this to her?"

"My soul knows and God knows it. I believe they will bring this up with her at some point." The brightness of her belief speaks of her confidence.

Tiyasha always remembers the person and she does her duty with devotion, diligence and delight.

We sat on the grass of our office lawn.

"Today we need to celebrate, right?" I said, and was waiting for Tiyasha's reply.

"Yes, obviously, come to our house today." Divya said, coming from behind. " We have not had any get-togethers for a long time. Please, can we do it today? We'll be back today in same shift also."

"Okay. I will take Ananya also. She can play with Shravya." I agreed with Divya, but Tiyasha did not utter a word.

She was busy in wearing a crepe bandage on her leg.

"Will you go or not? You are not even a part of our conversation." I asked Tiyasha while waiting for her reply.

"Yes.", she agreed but spoke in a very low voice.

"What happened to your leg?"

" I suddenly felt pain in my leg during the match."

"Oh. Have you applied pain relieving spray on the painful area?"

"Yes. But it is still not reducing my pain."

"Take one pain killer at night before sleeping." Divya said.

"Yes re. I am thinking of taking it to reduce my pain", she said to her teammate with a smile.

Divya left with the other team members.

"Tiash, I have seen you for many years. I have seen you dedicate your every success and happiness to a person? How such a dedication is possible?"

"It's dedication without any expectation. I remember the story of "Eklavya". This mythological character is my favorite. His dedication makes me realize the power of dedication. I focus only on the part of his dedication. If you see, he performed his duty with genuineness and respect towards his Guru. He never cared what would happen next or whether his Guru would know about him or not, or whether his Guru would reward him or not?

This dedication is not only limited to a single relationship as mentioned in the story. According to me, this dedication is required for any type of relationship or of work.

Dedication, consistency, focus, and willpower are the four pillars upon which I perform the duties of my life, and for me it is a token of respect towards her and her work, from my soul."

"I follow my favorite painter, but I am not a painter as I don't have the talent. How could I apply his thought process to my work as I am a pharma professional." I explained my point to my friend.

"If you truly want to apply, you should thoroughly examine his work style, words, and what he wants to convey through his paintings; concentrate on his hard work and dedication to his passion; and comprehend his thought process and the message he leaves through his work for his followers, and our society."

Amalgamate it with your profession, pick up the message from his painting. Suppose he expressed the pains of a father, then focus on the pain your father feels and why is he feeling the pain. You concentrate on yourself first. You focus on yourself first: are you the reason of your father's pain, and what actions of yours have made your father unhappy? Start introspection. Make it your aim to transform yourself slowly but steadily to make your dad happy. If the pain is not similar to the painting, at least you understand the pain of a father. You try to reduce his pain by improving yourself. Now, who is the person who cultivated the seeds of improvement within yourself?"

"My favorite painter." I found the answer, "What about my profession?"

"You meet many people in your profession. You will hear from them that their dad doesn't listen to them or they had an argument. Then go and talk to him. Understand what is exactly going on. The cause of his father's pain might be different from yours. Give him your example just to make him understand how you tried to improve yourself to reduce the pain of your father.

This way, at least you are making an attempt to comprehend your favorite painter's message and putting it into action through your efforts, as well as passing the message to others. You are respecting his efforts through your work.

And…as a pharmaceutical professional, when you solve your problem with your dad, you are happy. Your happiness leads to increase your focus on your work. You will work dedicatedly and try to minimize the chances of errors. .

Similarly, the person you assisted will concentrate on his work with a stress-free mind. Better productivity with better quality will improve the lives of our patients.

Finally, you aim to respect the work of your favorite painter by saying to yourself, "I will try to take care of the pains of others and find a way to reduce them by improving myself. I will help them so that they can cope with their pain independently. I will become their helping hand and not a dependent factor. I will try to minimize their pain in best possible way." Tiyasha finished answering my question.

"Let's go." she said to me.

"Hmmm…" I stood up, "Just the way sun does for the people, it rises, it shines, makes others shine. If my soul connects with the sun, then only will I understand the messages of the sun towards us. Then I first work on the message for myself later go to others.

This message of the sun is always present within my soul, and my soul is inseparable from me.

For me, Sun is that painter. I connect with his paintings from my soul. That's why I love his painting.

I should not only see the painting, I need to understand the inner meaning and start to work upon it with dedication, consistency, concentration, and will power. When I work, I will shine and help others to find the shining rays of their lives.

This sun never sets; it always rises within my soul as the sun is the creator of the creation. The sun and his creation are constant and continuous. His creation connects my soul, which, in turn connects many souls. So, he is the Sun of the souls of this world.

"I now understood, my friend." I smiled and extended my

hand to help her get up from the grass.

"Sun is closely related to the entity of my soul. Each and every expression of her words and her music are now embedded in the background of my thoughts." She says this for the person, who is the Sun of her soul and of many.

Tiyasha's each and every word reflects a high regard for the temperament of the sun of her soul.

Our favorite creative personality and his or her creation make us understand the value of his or her own creation as well as of others. He or she teaches us to respect all creative personalities and their creations and to understand its significance. Our favorite creative personality teaches us the value of team spirit and how to value your success with a balanced approach.

2011

BEAUTY OF UNIVERSAL TRUTH

"Hey, what are you doing?"

Tiyasha turned back and smiled at me.

"Enjoying a soul-soothing sunset, Anish."

"This splendid view of sunset makes me understand the importance of sunrise." I said.

"Sunrise and sunset are the truth of the Universe. We can never see the natural beauty of day and night without these two beautiful universal truths. Sunset and Sunrise speak to us every day. We need to adore both the sweet and bitter flavors of things to understand the true beauty of life." Tiyasha sipped her coffee.

"Hey, what's up? What are you thinking?"

I noticed her in deep thoughts. She was still holding her cup of coffee.

"Nothing important as such. But still thinking about something."

"Leave your "nothing and something". Just tell me – what are you thinking?"

"Nothing serious, buddy. Let me bring my companion."

"Companion?" I asked curiously. She went to the next

room to get her companion. She played the song "**Bothjhurir Dolnataay**", from the Bengali music album "Chupkatha". She came back with her mobile in her hand.

"Okay, madam. You carry on spending time with your companions. I have some pending office work."

"Which work re?"

"Need to prepare the list of product manufacturing activities to be completed by the end of this week."

I brought my diary and sat on the sofa. Tiyasha was engrossed in capturing photographs from the balcony of my room.

The mountains surrounded by trees and houses, ups and downs of roads, chilly evening and calm weather, the lights coming from faraway houses and spreading all over the area; this is Sikkim and the view of this mountainous terrain is a wonder of nature.

TREASURE OF A LIFE

Tiyasha was checking her phone.

"Hey, please make a cup of tea for me, naa, Tiash." Tiyasha walked towards the kitchen.

"Sorry. You will waste your energy on me for my tea." I said while she was moving towards the kitchen.

She blew on my head and went to the kitchen.

Tiyasha loves photography. I have seen many photographs captured by her, which are mostly of nature.

"If you understand nature, you will understand people, their silent and spoken words." Tiyasha told me.

"Bahinī, mailē mērō adhurō adhyayanakō lāgi bharnā garēm" ("Sister, I took admission for my incomplete studies", in the local language of Sikkim.), Parineeti said to Tiyasha.

Parineeti was from Sikkim and she ran her own restaurant. We went there quite often. She lost her father when she was very young. She did not complete her college studies as she needed to take care of her family.

"Anish, she is very focused on her bucket list. She could not complete her studies due to unfavorable circumstances. Whenever she gets the opportunity, she tries to fulfil her wishes.",

Tiyasha was telling me, at the canteen during our tea-break.

"Our friendship, staying away from home, our work - these are not the only our parts of life. We go to different places for work purpose, meet many people and get close to them. We make them a part of our lives unknowingly. We try to understand their nature, try to be with them when they need us. They try to be with us, whenever we need them. They play their part in our lives. This part of our life gives birth to many experiences and become our teachers. Overall, they are the treasure of our lives." Tiyasha shared her realization.

Tiyasha helped many boys and girls in their studies by helping them with their home work after coming back from company. She helped Parineeti and her brother, when they asked her. I always saw my friend busy before their examinations.

"When I hear Di's music, it reminds me of these people and their lives. I try to understand the significance of her songs. Her impactful singing makes me feel an urge to do something for them in my own possible way. Many raindrops of hope appear in front of my eyes, and Di's song creates a ray of inspiration in my thinking. I try to help them so they can create the rainbows of their lives."

We call our elder sister "Di". Tiyasha addressed Di as the best person in the world. She is another name for sisterhood for Tiyasha.

"Sir, your tea is ready. Please have it."

"Show me the snaps." I was taking a sip of tea made by her.

I love to have tea made by her as she prepares it as per my taste.

"Nice photography."

"The view of Sikkim is beautiful; I just captured this beauty. I don't have any credit here; all credit goes to God."

PREDICT UNPREDECTIBILITY

"Anish, I need to stay back till 7 pm today as I need to complete some pending tasks for tomorrow." I am at Tiyasha's desk, waiting for her boss, as he is not in his cabin.

Our journey began with this organization in Sikkim and evolved into an unbreakable love and friendship.

"Okay. Where is Sir, re?"

"In a meeting, perhaps."

I came for the second shift. I will leave by 11.00 pm. Tiyasha was on general shift. She leaves by 6 pm as per the shift timings.

"Receive all issued documents, check and put your signature on this tracker." Her words broke my chain of thoughts. She said to Amit, one of our colleagues.

I checked the time and it is 5:47 pm. I left for my work area.

I came to my documentation office from the product cubicle and I felt a sudden tremor.

"What are you doing here, man?" asked Ayan, my colleague, pulling my hand and running.

I heard my colleagues were screaming outside. Ground of our office building was shaking. I was clueless about what was going on. It felt like our office building would collapse.

"What is going on, yaar?"

"An earthquake struck Sikkim."

We hurriedly tried to get out of the building. It was very difficult as we were feeling tremors. Our staff was running. Their aprons, head gears were scattered here and there. Everyone was running to save their lives. Many were not able to maintain balance as the building was shaking.

I never had such an experience before. We were crossing the steps of the stairs. I stood sometimes as it felt like the floor of the building was bending.

Somehow, we managed to come out. All the employees were standing outside with fearful faces..

"Anish, where is Tiyasha?" asked Manali, who worked with her.

I was appalled.

"Where is she means? Did she not come out with you?"

"I just ran outside. I forgot to check on her."

I was not able to express what I was feeling. I was checking my phone. There was no network. What to do?

I ran towards the entrance of our building.

"Sir, don't go inside." The security officer opposed me entering the building.

"Daju (elder brother in the language of Sikkim), Tiyasha madam, is inside. She did not come out. I need to go to her department."

"Sir, don't get panicked. I am checking."

"Anish, she is coming out." Ayan came to me.

I saw her coming from the backside of our warehouse.

"Hey, what were you doing inside, Tiash?" I shouted at her.

"Chill," she said, holding my arms as I was losing patience.

"I was at my work desk. I didn't understand what was going on. I sat under my table. I was not able to run as I was feeling that I would fall down."

I did not know what to say.

"Hmm..."

We came from the office on foot. We were unable to contact our family.

We reached near Tiyasha's home around 9 pm. We saw Parineeti and her little daughter. They stood on the footpath in front of the restaurant. Andrew, her brother and many other people were also there.

People were not going in their houses as there was a high alert for the earthquake that may hit one more time. They planned to spend the night on the footpath, some of them planned to spend the night in the shop or garage, located on the roadside.

People chose a place from where they could immediately come out if earthquake were to hit again.

This was our life: power cut, water shortage, difficulty in obtaining food, no network, spending the night on a footpath, light rain, cold weather, and the fear of an earthquake.

Tiyasha hugged Aparna, the cute little daughter of Parineeti.

"She cried first, bahini. I ran outside by holding her on my lap. She started to laugh", Parineeti was telling Tiyasha.

"She must have felt that you were playing with her. It's good that she did not get panicked like us."

"Tiyasha, you can stay here tonight." said Poonam Thapa, mother of Sameer Thapa, to her. Sameer and her family stayed near Tiyasha's room, at Manipal. Tiyasha stayed in a rented room, near Manipal.

We all went in their garage. She spread a carpet over the floor and we all sat. It was 11:45 pm. We were eating biscuits. I was not able to go to my room as it was very far from here, that is, Manipal. I stayed near MG Marg, Gangtok.

"Anish, we need to predict unpredictability. Death is unpredictable, but it is true. I predict that unpredictability will come to me anytime. What to do?

If we are not there, the sun would still rise. In the same way, if I was not there, the sun of many souls would rise. So, till then I am on this earth and just cherishing my life through the rays of my sun. These build a dare to die attitude inside me and tells me to just do my work for myself and for others. Predicting unpredictability makes you focus more on your unfinished dreams."

One side building and another side hill – we are in between. If an earthquake strikes again, either the building or the hill rocks could collapse. I was about to tell this to my friend when I saw her sleeping with her juniors, her notebook, and the song, **"Sahaj premer gaan sonabo"** (from the Bengali music album "Chupkatha"). Tiyasha has many juniors wherever she goes, and I have many seniors wherever I go. They fell asleep, and I am still awake.

Tiyasha always tries to stay when she meets the unpredictability of life – by making others smile most of the time, sometimes by making fun of the particular situation through conversation, until this unpredictability does not break her from inside. When the unpredictability breaks her down, she plays the music of her Di and is lost in listening, trying to stand on her own feet, by being silent and concentrating on her passion or profession.

LIFE SOOTHING BREEZE

When I fell asleep, I could not sense anything. I checked my phone. The battery was running low.

How could I charge my mobile? Still there was power cut in the area. . Let me check if I can find out a way.

I got up from the carpet and saw Tiyasha standing on the road. I checked the time and it is 4:37 am.

"What are you doing here, Tiash?"

"Nothing. I just woke up. Did you not feel a slight jolt just two hours ago?"

"No. I fell asleep yaar."

"Good, at least you slept otherwise you would not be able to handle the circumstances. I heard that evening's magnitude was very high at 6.9 M. We will feel slight tremors quite often as we are in the range of the Himalayas."

"What are you saying? What to do now?"

"We can do nothing. Just watch the actions of nature. We can decide only after that. Residents of other regions near Sikkim also felt jolts from the earthquake."

"Hmm." A scary feeling was going inside me.

"Mom and dad will get tense by watching the news. We cannot even contact them as there is no network here.", Tiyasha was worried for them.

Suddenly, she said, "Anish, at least attend aunty's and dada's call. They always wait for you and your call. They are always there for you in any situation in your life. Without them, you will feel alone in this world."

I felt talking to them eagerly.. I recalled the mistake I had committed on 31st of December, 2009. I realized how much pain and stress we undergo when we don't hear from our family members' even for a single day.

I agreed with my friend.

We went back inside the garage. People were still sleeping.

I am listening to the song "**Jhochhona te mon**", from the Bengali music album "Chupkatha".

Tiyasha had downloaded songs in her mobile in the memory card, by going to a cybercafé near her room in Sikkim while coming back from our office. We did not get the music CDs from the shops. These were the days when we did not have an android mobile or laptop.

But, these things never stopped Tiyasha from listening to the songs, when she stayed out of her home town.

We, the listeners of music, have a deep sense of gratitude towards the creators of music. Amidst critical situations, when we are not able to think strategically, when we are not able to contact our loved ones, we feel alone, they become life soothing breeze for us.

'**Hay re Mon**' was playing from the same Bengali music album 'Chupkatha' on my friend's mobile.

A WISH = INNER STRENGTH FOR LIFETIME

"Bhai, Ciyā khānu, ('Have tea' in the local language of Sikkim)", Sameer offered me a cup of tea.

"Thank you, Daaju."

"Timrō sāthī kahām cha" Daju asked me in his language, "Where is your friend"?

I saw Tiyasha talking to Poonam aunty. "She is there with your mom." I pointed my finger at them to show Daju. Sameer went there to give them tea.

"Tiash, did you see the sunrise?" I also went to her.

"Yes. You already know that I love to see the first rays of dawn."

"Yes. But it is really difficult for me to wake up so early just to watch the sunrise every day, that too in the chilling weather of this place."

"I love to watch this, so I get up. I watch how the world changes from its night mode to light mode. I see how the darkness of night disappears and the world is filled with light by the first rays of the sun. The first sunrays of the day removes all darkness and spreads light all around. I like to witness this beauty of the Universe every day."

"What next? Shall we return to your room?"

"Yes. Let's go."

I remembered that my mobile needs to charge. Tiyasha's mobile phone battery was also running low.

We heard the news of many casualties and that the rescue officers are on their mission to save lives.

We saw many people taking shelter in the temple. Among them, were our friends from office and friends from other offices too. Some of them brought their families also. Many buildings had cracks in their walls, and some were slightly bent from the ground. Vehicles were almost not to be seen on the road.

We were getting off the stairs from Parineeti's house. Tiyasha suddenly stopped walking.

"What happened re?" I asked.

"Nothing."

" What's the matter?"

"Can I ever have the opportunity to hear the sun of my soul live in my life?"

"Hey…. Tiash,"

I was about to lose my balance.

She shouted at me, "Buddy, sit down immediately and don't run."

Tiyasha came forward as I panicked but she lost her balance.

I saw her sliding down from the steps. I screamed but was not able to understand what to do. Stones were rolling down from the surrounding hills. She was trying to save her head from colliding with the steps.

We felt sharp jolts; they came all of a sudden, threatened our lives and went away. When the situation got back to normal, Andrew, Parineeti and some others came to help my friend to make her stand. Her body was shaking. I brought water for her.

She saved her head, but injured her back, leg, and hand. She stopped herself by holding the side railings of the stairs. It was very difficult for her as she was standing in the center of the stairs while she was sliding down.

I could recall that she was struggling to hold the railing as the floor of the steps were itself shaking due to the jolts of the earthquake.

We immediately took her to the doctor. All the medical tests were done.

The doctor prescribed her rest for 10-20 days. She sprained her back and left leg and had many scratches all over her body.

Doctor Ramdin told us, "The way she fell down could have led to serious injury or even death. But she had some minor injuries as per God's will. It will take time for her to recover completely. She will feel pain while walking and moving. If she takes proper rest and has medicine, then she will be absolutely fine within a month."

I assured Tiyasha's mom, "Aunty, you don't worry, we are here to take care of your daughter."

"And mom, it will not be possible to come now as it will take some time for transport to be operational." Tiyasha said in a loud tone, so aunty can listen.

We will never forget those days when Andrew, Parineeti, Sameer, Poonam Aunty and many of Tiyasha's juniors were taking care of her completely.

Jolts are normal now as they occur anytime.

It took many months for everything to get back to normal, after this massive hit of nature. Our office building was severely damaged due to earthquake. By the God's grace, all of our officemates were safe.

Tiyasha completely recovered after about a month. What exactly did she say?

On the next day of the accident, we had a conversation. Andrew and Tiyasha's two or three juniors were there.

She was listening to the song, **"Tumi aasbey bole"** from the Bengali movie "Ranjana Ami ar ashbona".

"What is going to happen?" I asked her, as I was getting nervous to see her condition and surroundings after the earthquake.

"A new adventurous love story will be created between Anish Mukherjee and his wife. This earthquake hit love story will be broadcast through his own radio to his grandchildren at his old age." She gave me a serious reply and stared at me.

"Eh?" I was startled by her reply, "Who is my wife, re?"

"Find her. You are getting enough time now to find her and to reduce the stress of my aunty." she replied in a serious tone.

"I am getting tense. And you are making fun of me."

"Nothing will happen, dear. How could anything happen? Anish."

"I will hear the song of my soul live in my hometown.", She said firmly.

"If it is not possible, what will happen then?"

"I believe it will be, and if it isn't, I will continue with my work to make my life and the lives of others better and brighter, with immense love, respect, and strong belief in the sun of my soul."

Simple small wishes, but sometimes they are not fulfilled easily as we think. But these wishes become so important to a person that they turn out to be a source of their inner strength to face any situation in life. We can try to overcome all of our fears with a smile and a constructive mindset if we have a strong belief in our inner strength.

Tiyasha remembers the sun of her soul even in this cloudiness of her life.

The significance of a person in someone's life is understood when he or she remembers that person in tough times. By remembering that person, he or she defeats the fear against the odds.

Take care of your scare, bear its unbearable pain. You will become the fear to the scare of your life.

2010

THE CORE OF WILL POWER

"Go with them for boat paddling. Take dad also.", Tiyasha encouraged her mom to enjoy the trip with us.

"Mom, I will read books. I have music running in my veins. You know that these are my favorite activities. If I am not going doesn't mean, you will also not go." She tried to convince her parents to go for paddling.

"From tomorrow, we will return to our daily routine. Why do we need to waste our precious time in life by thinking about the past? Please go naa, Dad."

Finally, uncle and aunty were convinced to go with us for the trip.

"Oye, please take care of them. Don't keep your mobile on silent." Tiyasha instructed me with a smile.

We, Tiyasha and her parents, me and my mom, Mayank and his family, went to Nainital, another beautiful hill station, This 'Lake District' is a famous tourist spot in our country.

Dada did not come with us as he had his office work and our book store was also one of the reasons for not coming with us.

We came from Sikkim: Tiyasha, Mayank and Me. Mom came from Vizag to Kolkata. Then she came along with Tiyasha's parents from there. Mayank was our ex-colleague from Tripura. His mom, dad and wife, came from their native place.

We took a few days off from work to recharge our batteries so that we could be back with renewed energy at our workplace.

"We will walk." Tiyasha's dad and Mayank's dad told us yesterday while coming back to the hotel from the local market.

Tiyasha and her mom were about to leave by rickshaw. Mom and I also booked a rickshaw for us.

Mayank, his mom and wife, were still shopping at the local market.

We headed for our hotel by rickshaw. Tiyasha and aunty were following us in another rickshaw.

"Babu, where will you go?"

"We have planned for boat paddling. Let's see whether there are any other places we can visit. "

"Nainital is a beautiful place for sightseeing. How mesmerizing the view is.", Mom was admiring the beauty of the place.

My phone rang, it was Mayank's dad.

"Hello Uncle, Where are you?"

"We have taken Tiyasha to a hospital."

I was shocked.

"Whaaaaat? What happened to her?"

"You come here quickly.", Uncle's voice was shaking.

"Okay. We are coming."

I could feel my hands freezing. I didn't understand whether it was due to what I just heard or the cold weather.

'Tiyasha's scarf, which she wore around her neck, got stuck in the wheels of the rickshaw. She was not aware of it. When she realized it, she tried to pull the scarf from her neck as she was not able to breathe.", Aunty told me when I reached the hospital. I noticed her hands were shaking while telling me about the incident.

"I was sitting beside her, Anish, but not able to do anything. I saw her falling down from the rickshaw as she lost her senses." I was feeling the dolorous pain of a helpless mother, sitting beside her daughter, seeing her child going through a life threatening stage.

Mayank's dad and your uncle were walking behind the rickshaw. They saw and ran towards us. They managed to pull out the scarf around Tiyasha's neck with the help of a passerby. She got back to her senses that moment, but was not able to move due to the pain in her neck. The guy was very helpful and brought Tiyasha here in his car, without wasting a single moment.", Aunty continued.

"What did the doctor say?", I queried.

"We managed to bring her in the nick of time. She has got a clot around her neck." Aunty sighed.

"And ...it looks like a necklace, actually half a necklace. So, from now on I won't need any neck ornament. It will save money.", We heard Tiyasha's voice.

We turned and saw her with a bandage around her neck. She also had swelling on the shoulder.

"Let's go dad. I am fine." Tiyasha was ready to go back to the hotel, "Thank you Sir for your help."

She thanked Sanjeev, the guy who helped to bring her to the hospital.

"It is okay. Take care of yourself, Tiyasha. Do you need me to drop at your hotel?"

Sanjeev stayed in Nainital. He owned a printing press.

"No, it's okay. I will walk down with Anish. If it's convenient for you, you can drop my parents to the hotel."

"Yes, surely. I will drop them." He said happily.

"How will you walk? You come with us." Tiyasha's dad said to her.

"Dad, I am fine. I have only injured my neck and shoulder and not my leg. I just need some fresh air. ", She explained.

"Uncle, all of you go with Sanjeev. We will come. I am here with Tiyasha."

Uncle initially disagreed but finally relented.

"Dad, inform me when you reach the hotel.", Tiyasha said.

"Okay. But take care." Uncle finally agreed to leave with Sanjeev.

They left by car and we started to walk. Walking along the mountain road took about 40-45 minutes.

We reached our hotel. Uncle informed us on reaching the hotel.

"Anish, you go inside. I want to sit here." She sat on the bench, staring at the sky.

"What happened?"

"I want to sit here alone. I want to see the evening view of the sky and want to listen to the song of Di."

I understood that Tiyasha wanted to spend some alone time. She played the song, **"Mon hawa te"** from the Bengali music album "Chupkatha". It was 6:17 pm.

We returned to our respective places from the Nainital trip. Tiyasha's parents returned to Sikkim with her and my mom also did the same.

Tiyasha went to see Doctor Manoj to begin regular treatment for the wounds in her neck. He cleaned the blood that had been deposited in the wound before dressing it. Almost after 15 days, it started to heal. Tiyasha still has a light scar around her neck as it was a very deep wound.

Tiyasha is the boxer in the ring of a life—sometimes the situations of life knock her down, sometimes she knocks them down. She plays fairly and dedicatedly and punches the situations of life back through the tough situations of life.

"Defeat knocks at my door, and I open the door. It knocks me out and gives me an opportunity to revise my skills and update new skills. It gives me time to think about myself, so I can checkmate defeats from the next time."

Her undivided reliance on the sun of her soul creates her willpower.

Design the root cause of your defeat, so that you can design the new roots of your success.

2022

MUSIC OF A PURE SOUL

"Nish, what are you thinking?" Ananya came to the balcony of Tiyasha's home. I was standing and walking down the lanes of thrilling memory.

I was remembering some of the days among many rough and tough ones. When I think of those days, I realize that music and its creators can never be separated from us.

Tiyasha Roy is taking rest as she is finding it difficult to walk or move for the last four days.

After the match, she was feeling pain in her leg and it got swollen. We went to see a doctor when the pain increased. A blood clot was found in the veins of her leg.

Doctor Rajiv said, "As it is diagnosed early, it will be recovered soon. We simply need to ensure that blood clots do not travel to the lungs. Then it will be critical."

"How did it happen, doctor?" Tiyasha asked.

"Blood clots may be formed from any type of injury."

Rajiv advised her, "You take medicine and use the compression stockings."

"What is Mani doing re?"

"She is writing something and listening to music."

" Come with me.", I took her to the room of my friend.

Mom was staying with Tiyasha at her home. Ruma managed our house for Ananya and me.

Ananya spends most of her time with her senior. Last night, aunty and uncle reached Vizag.

Everyone is sitting in the dining room, watching television and having "Onion Pakoda," "Aloo Pakoda," and coffee.

"Oye, what are you doing?"

"Writing my parts in your story." Tiyasha replied to me.

"Tiash, why you did not tell everyone that the clot might become critical if it moved to the lungs?"

"Anish, you only said the word 'if'. That means I am fine and there is no 'if'. I am taking medicines. It will soon be fine. The size of the clot is also a prime factor here."

"Hmmm"

"As per the medical test reports, it is not too big."

"Hmmm."

In the middle of our conversation, Ananya plays the song **"Beshure"**, from the Bengali movie "Mini".

"Tiash, our star is shining with the music of the sun of your soul."

"Because the sun of my soul is also the music of a pure soul. Her song connects the souls of generations to generations."

NEVER ENDING REALITY

Anish tells me to give a brief introduction. How could I introduce myself?

I am Tiyasha Roy and this is my only introduction.

We are all doing fine in our individual lives and in our cumulative lives also. Anish and I manage our enjoyable work-life balance with our star and other family members, obviously with music, with the sun of the souls and her songs, along with different creations of different creative personalities.

Every day we go through new journeys in our lives, new battles in our lives, we meet new acquaintances. We welcome them. Some old pages will be deleted, new pages will be added, and some old pages will be modified. This is our life cycle. This lifecycle would be meaningless without the creation and its creators. We are the pilgrims of this never ending process, so our stories also.......

You are the first radio station I listen to in the morning;

You are the cup of coffee of my tiring days;

*You are the focal point of the strength of concentration in the
 distracted moments of my life;*

You are the inhaler of my life's mountainous roads;

You are the password to the inaccessible journey of my life.

You are the never-ending reality of my soul.......

You are the never-ending reality of many souls.......

You are the sun of our souls......